The Subconscious Mind: An Untapped Data Bank

Loretta Flock Thom

Study In Depth

The Subconscious Mind: An Untapped Data Bank

By

Loretta Flock Thom

University of Oklahoma

Dr. Jorge L. Mendoza

Psychology Department

Bachelor of Liberal Studies: Administrative Leadership Concentration

November 1, 2000

University of Oklahoma

Abstract

The Subconscious Mind: An Untapped Data Bank

By Loretta Thom

The subconscious mind is a discussion by many experts in various fields, such as Psychology, Epistemology, Neurology, Metaphysics, Philosophy, Theology, and Alternative Medicine. This author will focus on the subconscious as a viable source of knowledge that we have yet to use to even it's minor potential, and put forth the following theories:

The subconscious or super subconscious is an entity of universal knowledge that could be used as a communication tool. It is not limited to the connection from our own subconscious to our conscious. The subconscious mind and its parts allow us to communicate and connect with all living things in existence. This connection could be an infinite source of information about the past, present and future. This aspect would be of use in all these fields mentioned above as well as all other types of quests for knowledge and understanding.

Study in Depth Introduction

The Subconscious Mind: An Untapped Data Bank

Man's search for knowledge is an infinite quest. Has the ultimate source for knowledge been found but ignored? Is all knowledge within our grasp if we open our mind to its existence and capabilities? "Carl Jung said that archetypes hold past knowledge and the subconscious mind holds all of mans past archetypical images as well as beliefs (Cox, D. 1968, pg. 138)." Other experts in this field believe that there is a universal consciousness and being universal, it could hold the accumulation of all knowledge that the mental capacity has obtained as well as knowledge waiting to be obtained. "The mind is capable of anything-because everything is in it, all past as well as future (Joseph Conrad as cited in Sagan, C. 1977. pg. 198)."

The subconscious mind: an untapped data bank is a subject about communicating with a part of ourselves that is a part of a larger whole. In researching the data needed for writing on this subject, it was found that many authors have varying theories on this subject. However, they all have a common link in believing that there does exist a vast amount of knowledge that we do not utilize.

Sigmund Freud was known for his work with the psychological, dreams, and the personality. He was instrumental in paving the way for his successors and their theories. This author found his views on man and the conscious valuable in the beginnings of the research for this paper. Some of his followers such as Carl Jung played a deeper role in emphasizing the theory of the subconscious and its levels being a vast untapped source of knowledge.

Ernest Holmes book "The Science of the Mind" gave further data and was a great source of information. He stated in this book the limitless potential of the subjective mind. He also offered the theory of their being a universal mind.

Since this is a theory this author came up with before reading their works, it was somewhat of a surprise to find so many commonalities between, Carl Jung, Sigmund Freud, Joseph Murphy, Ernest Holmes, Alice Bryant, and over 50 others in different areas of study having the same conception on the conscious and subconscious that this author started out trying to express. That in its self showed this author that the theory had merit. If so many people including this author came to the same conclusion at different times in history, all from different walks of life, and environment, then this showed a universal mind was at work.

Exploration into the possibilities of the subconscious mind and its connection between each living thing will be investigated along with the vast potential contained within the subconscious. This connection would provide an interchange of knowledge between men, other living creations, as well as with the great creating force of the universe. The paper will view aspects of this theory from scientific, psychological, metaphysical, philosophical, and historical standpoints.

The Subconscious Mind: An Untapped Data Bank

Opinions on What the Subconscious Is.

The subconscious mind, according to many theorists, is a term given to describe part of the mind that stores past experiences and feelings, as well as a source of unexplained, unproven, or unaware ideas and thoughts that man has experienced. "No simple agreed upon definition of consciousness exists. Attempted definitions tend to be tautological (for example, consciousness defined as awareness) or merely descriptive (for example, consciousness described as sensations, thoughts, or feelings) (Consciousness, States of, Microsoft Encarta, 2000, *Introduction*, pg. 1)."

Sigmund Freud believed it held repressed memories or experiences. "He suggested that the unconscious mind is where material is kept that is not readily available to us such as fears and unpleasant memories (Pettijohn, T. F. 1992, pg. 106)." Freud felt that the unconscious held primarily instinctual material.

He stated that the conscious system is derived from both instinctual material and perception. Instinctual material that is present in the conscious system has already passed through the unconscious system; in the conscious system it undergoes further development. Thus the conscious system receives material from the unconscious, but works that material over. Freud sums up his theory with the following words:

The content of the Unconscious may be compared with an aboriginal population in the mind. If inherited mental formations exist in the human being-something analogous to instinct in animals- these constitute the nucleus of the unconscious. Later there is added to them what is discarded during childhood development as unserviceable; and this need not differ in nature from what is inherited. A sharp and final division between the content of the two systems does not, as a rule, take place until puberty. (Rosenfield, I. 1970, pg.53-54).

This would indicate that children have a better connection than adults with their past as well as present. The process of instilled beliefs and behavior as we age decreases this connection from flowing as freely as it did when we were "uncorrupted" and filled with more innocence. There are many popular "sayings" that many of us have heard as we grew up regarding what and who will be able to tap into this knowledge bank. "Out of the mouths of babes," and "the little children will lead them," are just a couple that could be used to support the theory Freud had that the child before puberty has a strong connection with the subconscious and conscious. His theory of an original connection then a division of the consciousness included what the unconscious held, which as stated earlier, were instincts and memories.

Carl Jung believed that past experiences or memories could be passed from generation to generation and he called these archetypes.

The collective unconscious reflects the collective experiences that humans have had in their evolutionary past, or in Jung's own words, " it is the deposit of ancestral experience from untold millions of years, the echo of prehistoric world events to which each century adds an infinitesimally small amount of variation and differentiation ." (Jung as cited in Hergenhahn, B.R. 1990, pg. 69).

In the book "The Bible Readers Companion by Lawrence Richards, he quotes a scripture from "The Holy Bible" which backs up the theory of Carl Jung. Jung used his theory of archetypes to state that past memories and occurrences are inherited from one generation to the next.

> The thing that hath been, it is that which shall be; and that which is done is that which shall be done: and there is no new thing under the sun. Is there anything whereof it may be said, See, this is new? It hath been already of old time, which was before us. ((Ecclesiastes 1:9-10) Richards, L. 1991, pg. 398).

Many believe the subconscious mind to be a part of a whole. The belief is that it is not an individual entity but a universal power that can be tapped into by individuals. It is referred to in different ways, some call it a power, others a connection of spirit, and still others as past memories of ancestors being remembered. "The super-subconscious mind is the creative, intuitive, mental, image-making faculty within ourselves (2000, August 25, http://www.lightparty.com/Health/SuperSub.html)." One theory is that man was given all the knowledge he would ever need which is at his disposal at any time he wishes to understand and obtain it. "When man first appeared upon the earth he was endowed with all the creative forces of Nature. Only through neglect of this power can man be unhappy, ill, or burdened by poverty (Ferguson, R. 1979, pg 25)." Ernest Holmes believed that the source of this knowledge was from our creator. In the book "Science of the Mind' Holmes wrote:

> Man has at his disposal in what he calls his subjective mind, a power that seems to be limitless. This is because he is one with the whole on the subjective side of life. Man's thoughts falling into his subjective mind, merges with the Universal

Subjective Mind, and becomes the law of his life, through the one great law of life. (Holmes, E. 1998, pg. 29).

He believed this whole or universal mind to be God. His belief was that whatever we think is law, we make so in our lives as the only law.

The subconscious is not limited to human animals alone, many theorize that it exists in all animals. "No one can say for sure, but in the night all cats are black. And in the dark forests of the unconscious, all of us---beasts and humans---may look very much alike (Kowalski, G. 1991, pg. 28)."

The Native American believes in a oneness with man, nature, and the Great Spirit. They believe that communication between man and spirit is a common occurrence. "The Native Americans believed in communing with their ancestors and with plants, animals, and spirits (Hirschfelder, A. 2000, pg.19)." This could also be explained as a level of the subconscious being in communication with a greater power.

It is difficult to probe the inward awareness of another being. The realm of what one mystic called "the interior castle" is wholly private and wrapped in solitude. But, when we look into another's eyes—even into the eyes of an animal—we may find a small window into that inner sanctum, a window through which our souls can hail and greet one another. (Kowalski, G. 1991, pg. 84).

Plato referred to a knowledge outside of our conscious realm. Plato believed in two separate states of being, one of forms and one of appearances. "Plato argued that the reason for disagreements among people concerning truth was that they confused these two worlds; only the world of *Timeless Ideas* could produce true knowledge, whereas the world of appearances could produce only opinion (Stumpf, S. 1994, pg. 47)."

Aristotle had an opinion as to the origin of knowledge and wisdom. He believed that wisdom came from more than just repeated experiences.

There are different levels of knowledge. Some people know only what they experience through their senses, as for example, when they know that fire is hot. But, says Aristotle, we do not regard what we know through the senses as wisdom. To be sure, our most authoritative knowledge of particular things is acquired through our senses. (Stumpf, S. 1994, pg. 88).

Theoretically, the unconscious is a storage area for many different types of knowledge. It can hold past forms, ideas, archetypes, and memories. The unconscious is a means of tapping into a different plane of reality. We know that many humans experience things in the realms of their mind that has no valid explanation in the hard light of reality.

In the book "How to Think Like Leonardo da Vinci" a definition of consciousness is given as follows: *"Connessione* is a recognition of and appreciation for the interconnectedness of all things and phenomena (Gelb, Michael J. 1998, pg. 222)."

One of the generalized opinions offered by the layperson is that the subconscious is the inner thoughts that are kept beneath the surface of the conscious mind. It is conceived as a part of ourselves that we do not allow to come to the surface. Hidden thoughts, ideas or memories that we either consciously keep separate from our daily conscious thoughts, or ones that we have no control over and appear and disappear at will according to pressure from emotional or physical stimulus. "The Unconscious, in psychology, hypothetical region of the mind containing wishes, memories, fears, feelings, and ideas that are prevented from expression in conscious awareness (Consciousness, States of, Microsoft Encarta, 2000, *Unconscious*, pg. 1)."

This variety of beliefs is but a few written on what the subconscious is believed to be. Some think of it as limitless, others think of it as another aspect of ourselves, still others think of it as a connection with a greater power, and many are mystified as to what it is and what it contains.

In the end they are all theories and beliefs that have been put forth based on beliefs, experiences, experiments, and learned behavior. As Holmes said, for that person their theory of the subconscious becomes law. They do not explore any further and feel no need to because they are satisfied with the law they have developed. Knowledge cannot be obtained if no one is searching. This author puts forth the theory that the subconscious mind and its depths has unlimited potential to provide us with the knowledge we need in all areas of our life because it is a direct link with the creating force of the universe.

Categorizing the Subconscious.

According to the studies conducted to date, the potential of the subconscious has not been discovered.

Looked at on a pro-rata size per task responsibility function the "Subconscious mind appears to be, as is assumed to be worthy of the figure of 90-95%of your overall mind, with your Conscious mind being represented by the figure of 5-10%. (2000, August 25, http://www.ascc.org/library/art11.html). Figure 1 gives a visual representation of this percentage.

Red-Conscious   Brown-Subconscious

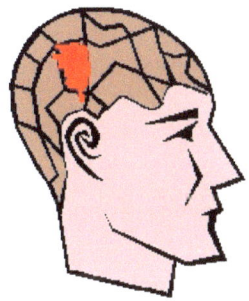

Fig.1

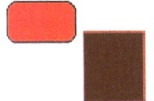

Thom, Loretta (2000). Designed by Clipart from Word and Coloring and Assembly by Loretta Thom.

This visual diagram shows the portion of the mind that is used, and the portion that is not. We only use a small portion of our mind. The subconscious portion of the brain and its potential has not been utilized to its fullest potential.

Pyotr Anokhin of Moscow University, a student of the legendary psychological pioneer Ivan Pavlov, staggered the entire scientific community when he published his research in 1968 demonstrating that the minimum number of potential thought patterns the average brain can make is the number 1 followed by 10.5 million kilometers of typewritten zeros. Anokhin compared the human brain to a "multidimensional musical instrument that could play an infinite number of musical pieces simultaneously." He emphasized that each of us is gifted with a birthright of virtually unlimited potential. And he proclaimed that no man or woman, past or present, has fully explored the capacities of the brain. (Gelb, M. 1998, pg.5-6).

How can the limited working capacity of the mind comprehend, reduce, and explain what it is not aware of? One example of this would be an isolated race of beings with their own centuries of traditions and beliefs trying to understand Christianity. First they must be made aware of an alternative way of believing, then be schooled on what the other belief entails. Upon completing this education, they have to decide whether or not to accept this way of thinking. Do they not understand the Christian God? Or do they simply not understand others views of a God? When a different belief is introduced, first it must be explained what is being introduced. This is the beginning of a belief system being reduced and categorized. It has to be put into a context that the other party can identify with. They relate it to something they already know. Thus their knowledge and past archetypes are now interwoven with their comprehension of this belief. It is now a changed or expanded explanation and definition of that divinity. Has this ever been necessary? It is a historical fact that all races of man have had a belief in a higher power.

In all cultures, human beings make a practice of interacting with what are taken to be spiritual powers. These powers may be in the form of gods, spirits, ancestors, or any kind of sacred reality with which humans believe themselves to be connected. Sometimes a spiritual power is understood broadly as an all-embracing reality. (Consciousness, States of, Microsoft Encarta, 2000, *Religion*, pg. 1).

Many of these forms of belief are similar. It is a universal pattern of thought that exists whether a society is integrated or isolated. Perhaps explanations and categorizations as to a higher power and how knowledge is obtained have never been necessary.

We are only aware of the aspect of the subconscious that we are able to experience. In the scientific sense, it is something that has to be tested. Aristotle is just one person who stated that scientists begin by looking at something, and then move on to think about the possible cause of the experience in question.

Carl Jung stated that the test person either doubts the possibility of knowing something one cannot know, or hopes that it will be possible and that the miracle will happen. At all events the test person being confronted with a seemingly impossible task finds himself in the archetypal situation which so often occurs in myths and fairy tales, where a divine intervention, i.e., a miracle, offers the only solution. (Nichols, S. 1984, pg. 48).

When an unknown exists, sooner or later a study is developed to find out what the unknown is, where it came from, and what caused its creation. There is a science for every area of investigation. Science allows us to take the unknown from a broad sense to a categorized entity and study it on a minuet basis. We break things down until they are at a point that we can understand and begin to study. How can you test something that has no boundaries and is open to all beliefs and ideas, past, present and future?

We can only test it in a limited sense because we are limiting it the moment we begin to put it within a frame or category. We want to box it up like a package and say, OK, this is what it is and this is what it does. In order to test it, you must decide what area you will test, what is a positive test result and what is a negative, what method is to be used as an accurate measure of the test and what is possible and what is not possible to test. You have already limited yourself before you begin. "The background of the creative act is a somehow desirable and proper mystery. It is a bit brash to undertake a scientific study of imagination and originality (Coopersmith, S. 1966, pg. 255)."

We are trying to test an entity with our current mental potential, which has preconceived beliefs, standards, and methods that we adhere to.

Where Would the Power of the Subconscious Come From?

Is the subconscious an entity that can be physically located? This is a study that has been going on for quite some time. We know that Plato and Aristotle had opinions on the subconscious, and this search for answers as to how the mind and subconscious works has continued. Renee Descartes, the French philosopher, began his studies of the mind in the 1700's. "Descartes asked: Is the mind, or consciousness, independent of matter? Is consciousness extended (physical) or unextended (nonphysical)? Is consciousness determinative, or is it determined (2000, October 26, http://encarta.msn.com/index/consciseindex/51/051E8000.htm?z=1&pg=2&br=1)?"

Many scientists, physicians, physiologists, philosophers, and other researchers in many fields have followed him. They have had many theories as to what it is, its relevance to the conscious mind, as well as where it originates.

A scientific world-view which does not profoundly come to terms with the problems of conscious minds can have no serious pretensions of completeness. Consciousness is part of our universe, so any physical theory which makes no proper place for it falls fundamentally short of providing a genuine description of the world. I would maintain that there is yet no physical, biological, or computational theory that comes very close to explaining our consciousness and consequent intelligence; but that should not deter us from striving to search for one. (Penrose, R. 1994, pg. 8).

Renee Descartes believed that it came from God. Freud believed it was a part of us that originates from past personal experiences. Carl Jung theorized that it was inherited archetypes held in the subconscious. This quote from "Jung and Tarot: An Archetypal Journey" is used to illustrate the infinite expanse of the subconscious and what depths may be held within it.

The physical universe is not the result of Original life power acting on matter, it is the result of life power acting upon itself. Out of itself the One Power builds all shapes and forms, all force, and myriad of structures. All things are from this One, by the meditation of The One, and all things have their birth from this One Thing. This expresses a truth on both the macrocosmic and the microcosmic planes of existence. (Nichols, S. 1984 p.47).

We are all from One and connected to The One. Therefore we have a link within us to communicate with all things because the same force creates all things. "The endowments that we possess are not of ourselves, but of God (Calvin as cited by Till, C.V. 1966 pg.87)."

On a biological level, many believe that our DNA passes memories down from one generation to the next.

According to the multimdimensionally aware, cellular (DNA) memory is very real. Emotions, especially traumatic experiences, embody at the cellular level and remain there to be passed on through genetic coding from generation to generation. Within every being, the memories of all ancestors reside, waiting for their chance to speak-and speak they will. Cellular memories enter into the ESP core and surface in the same manner as knowledge from the unified field. They are subject to the same routing as direct knowledge. They can enter consciousness as a complete, fully developed "knowing," or they can appear as visions, symbols or (inexplicable) feelings. (Bryant, A. & Seebach, L. 1998, pg. 204-205).

This theory would lead to the conclusion of our knowledge and subconscious residing within our cellular makeup.

"It is difficult for modern science to accept that consciousness and brain are to some extent independent of each other, and that during an out-of-body experience it is possible to gain accurate information not through the senses (Fenwick, P. & Fenwick E. 1998, pg. 260)." Why has the exact location of the subconscious not been located? This author believes it is because it is not a physical thing. It is an essence and assimilation of many things which all originate from one source. The subconscious has many facets such as archetypes, memories, and dreams. However, their abilities come from the same source and work together as a whole.

There is one Infinite Mind which of necessity includes all that is, whether it be the intelligence in man, the life in the animal, or the invisible Presence which is God. Anything anyone has ever done, anybody can do: there can be no secrets in nature. This I have always believed. There is no special providence, no God who says, "I am going to tell you what I didn't tell any others." There is a power for good in the universe greater than you are and you can use it. (2000, September 10, http://www.religiousscience.org/firstrs1.htm).

This power and Oneness is a common theme that has been put into many modern day movies such as "Star Wars," "The Empire Strikes Back," and "The Matrix." This theme is the idea of a force within ourselves that connects with the universe. In Star Wars, The Empire Strikes Back, and the rest of the Star War Episodes, the Jedi for the good learns to tap into this power and use it to know what others are thinking, move objects, and sense what is happening in other places. The Dark Forces have tapped into the same power, using it for evil and self-gain. In The Matrix, a select group of people realizes that their world is really not reality, but an instilled thought pattern being programmed into their minds. They can use the true power of their mind to escape from this alternate reality and fight against its creators. They are very entertaining movies, however, in reference to the common theme, it is one of connecting to a power already within themselves that is connected to a whole.

Ernest Holmes stated his opinion of this connection with a greater one in his book "Science of the Mind."

> When we know our Oneness with God and Law, what a great burden is removed. Any sense of opposition is removed from the consciousness which perceives Unity. That which we call OUR subjective mind is but a point in Universal Mind where our personality maintains its individualized expression of Spirit. If we think of ourselves as being separated from the Universe, we shall be limited by this thought, for it is a belief in separation from God which binds and limits. (Holmes, E. 1998, pg. 127-128).

These statements show the common belief in an ultimate creating power in the universe. This common belief is shown in the movies, the biology, and the spiritual sides of different forms of expression. Thus, these beliefs would tend to point to the location of the power of the subconscious coming from one great-connected entity in the universe.

Theory of Subconscious Communication

If the subconscious comes from one great entity that we are all connected to, and if there is nothing new under the sun, then great ideas could have been transported in this manner. This author believes that man has experienced this communication, and that we can communicate with each other and by doing so acquire knowledge others have. "Einstein stated that he never came upon any of his discoveries through the process of rational thinking (2000, August 25, http://www.higherawarebess.com/awarebessandintuition.shtml)." "Mozart stated in a letter to a friend that tunes simply floated into his head: "Where and how they come, I know not: nor can I force them" (Kowalski, G. 1991, pg. 35)." In the book "Modern Psychology: The Teachings of Carl Gustav Jung," the writer David Cox quotes Jung:

There are occasions when one can become conscious of elements of the collective unconscious and gain tremendous benefit from it, but that does not mean that those elements become part of consciousness. It is highly probable that great artistic work, great scientific discoveries and many other similar things result from the fact that elements of the collective unconscious press forward through consciousness, and in analytical experience people may be faced with the tremendous power of the contents of the collective unconscious. (Cox, D. 1968, pg. 89).

Where do we get our ideas? We get some from experience, acquired knowledge, instinct, and learned behavior. What about the ideas that we have that is totally out of our realm of experiences or thinking? According to some experts, it comes from a source outside of our conscious knowledge. How could universal transmission of this knowledge work?

If radio waves, energy, light, and other unseen atomic forces can travel through space and time, why not thought? "Advanced concepts often come to the multimdimensionally aware in the form of a universal communication system, carried by light, seen as visions, symbols, numbers or heard through unusual, and not yet quite understood, sound mechanisms (Bryant, A. & Seebach, L. 1998, pg. 6)."

Variations in consciousness are intimately related to changes in electrical activity in the brain. Investigators have been exploring this relationship ever since Hans Berger (1929) invented the EEG. The electroencephalograph (EEG) is a device that monitors the electrical activity of the brain over time by means of recording electrodes attached to the surface of the scalp. The EEG records and amplifies electrical activity in the outer layer of the brain, the cortex. (Weiten, W. 1997, pg.122).

You can see what brain waves look like in Figure 2 below:

Fig.2 (Weiten, W. 1997, pg. 126.)

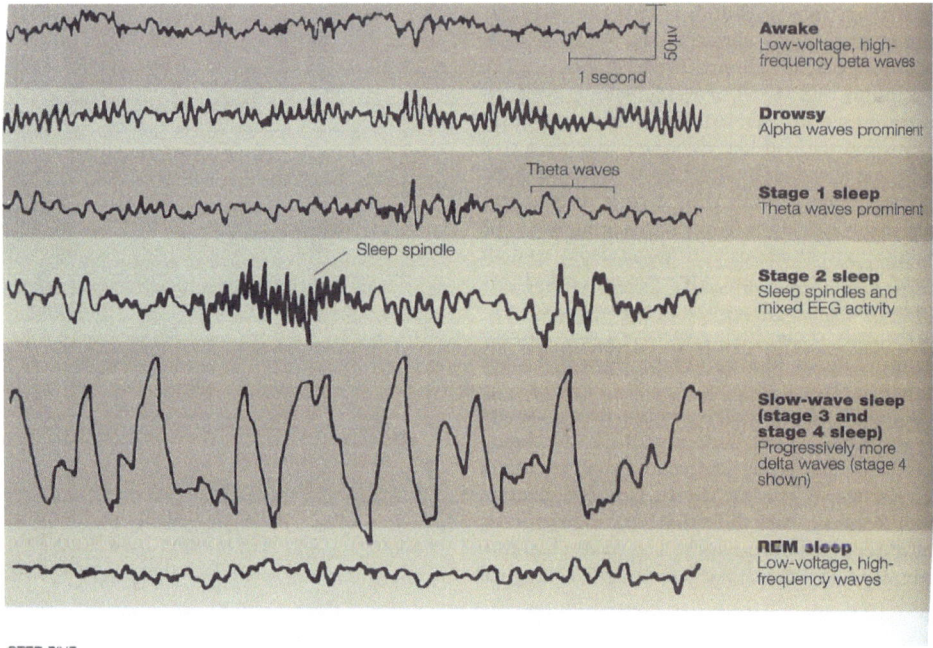

From: Weiten, W. (1997). <u>Psychology Themes and Variations 3rd Ed</u>. New York: Brooks/Cole Publishing. Pg. 126, Chart 5.5 EEG.

These brain waves show different stages of consciousness. It is shown that brain waves during REM sleep resemble wide-awake brain waves. If the brain waves are similar, then thought processes could be occurring while in a dream state. The theory for brainwave activity communication from one being to another is a very viable one. It has been proven in many instances that while asleep, the mind is given solutions to problems and warnings of future occurrences.

Figure 3 shows radio waves hitting a reflector of a radio telescope and being focused on the aerial and then sent to a recorder.

Fig. 3 (Groiler, 1967, pg. 71, vol. 16)

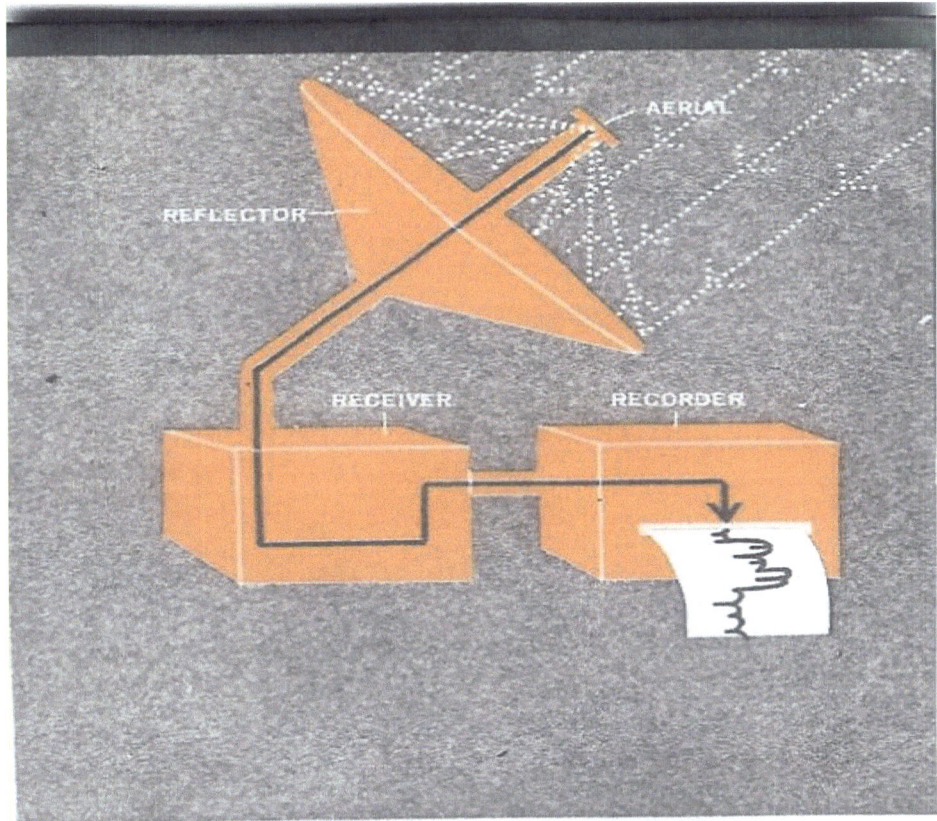

Radio waves striking the reflector of a radio telescope are focused on the aerial and then sent to a recorder.

The New Book of Knowledge: The Children's Encyclopedia. (1967) New York: Groiler. Vol. 16, pg. 71.

Our thoughts are formed into waves and can be transmitted to one another the same way as radio signals can be transmitted to a receiver. In the diagram above, simply think of two minds communicating in the same way through transmitted signals. The key is for the transmitter to be aware of incoming data and the receiver to be open to reception of this data. Telepathy is a well-known example of communication on a mental thought or wave pattern basis from one individual to another. Our preconceived beliefs and prior conditioning can become a blockage to this transmission.

Our religious beliefs can be a main source of acceptance or dismissal of past or future innovations. Subconscious communication, or communication from one mind to another is not something that is without merit in the religious sects of society. Christianity believes in one God. They believe the "Holy Bible" is the word of God. Christians believe that the books of the Bible were inspired by God and written by men. Does this not mean that an entity communicated with man through thought?

> The Bible points to God as its author; yet it was written by human hands; and in the varied style of its different books it presents the characteristics of the several writers. The truths revealed are all "given by inspiration of God" (2 Timothy 3:16): yet they are expressed in the words of men. The Infinite One by His Holy Spirit has shed light into the minds and hearts of His servants. He has given dreams and visions, symbols and figures; and those to whom the truth was thus revealed have themselves embodied the thought in human language. (White, E. 1971, pg. 9).

There are many passages in the Christian Bible that refer to a means of communication from a great creating force to man. One such scripture is "The words I say to you I do not speak of my own accord, but the Master Within does his works ((Jn. 14: 10) Martin, T. 1997, pg. 25)." This passage implies that the communication to our conscious comes from something that already resides within.

Whether it is religious, scientific, metaphysical, or biological; there is a common theory of communication from a deeper place within the mind to the outward conscious mind.

Stigma Attached to those Who Tap Into the Subconscious.

Throughout history there has been people who have been able to accurately tell a person about something in their past or foretell future events. Some of the most famous are Nostradamus, Edgar Cayce, and a slave fortune teller called Tituba in 1692. Nostradamus was a famous visionary. He was born Michel de Nostredame in Provence, France in 1503. His family was originally Jewish and then converted to Catholicism. He was well trained in many languages as well as astrology and medicine. He became a physician and is reputed to have created remarkable cures during outbreaks of the plague in France.

Nostradamus did not start to glimpse into the future until he was in his early forties. First he would receive premonitions and then experience visual flashes of insight. His rhymed prophesies, published under the title *Centuries* (1555), brought him the favor of the French court. (Robinson, L. & Finnerty, L. 1999, pg. 24).

Edgar Cayce is a 20th century American who is known for psychic healing.

He grew up on a farm near Hopkinsville, Kentucky. He discovered through his own illness, paralysis of the throat muscles, that he was able to lose consciousness at will and enter a deep hypnotic-like sleep state from which he could discourse physical conditions and recommend treatment for those who sought his help. (Sechrist, E. 1995, pg. Vii).

Tituba was a slave who confessed to being a witch at the Salem Witch Trials. These three are a good indication of stigma attached to people who practice the conception of tapping into a subconscious or higher power. Nostradamus was renowned and his quatrains were published by the French Court. Tituba was deemed a witch and put on trial. Edgar Cayce is considered nothing more than a popular entertainer to some and a true psychic to others.

People who have practiced different arts such as mind reading, fortune telling, prophesying or ESP are either sought after or shunned. Those that are genuine and believed are conceived as having a God given gift or in league with dark forces. If it is a message that is deemed angelic, then according to the beliefs of the audience, it is usually surmised to be sent from God. An example of this would be in a religious gathering where someone states they have a message given to them by God. It could be a message stating good reports or warnings of upcoming problems to be overcome. On the other side of the spectrum, if a message is of a displeasing nature, such as to imply negative thoughts about your current religion, some say it is from Satan or other evil personas. The people delivering these words of wisdom or prophecy have been named everything from prophets to witches.

What about those with futuristic wisdom such as Albert Einstein or Leonardo da Vinci? They were able to bring to light new ways of thinking and doing things. Einstein's physics was instrumental in opening the way for much of today's technology. Which category should genius fall into? Where does their great mental thought processes come from?

Scientific research reveals that you probably underestimate your own capabilities. You are gifted with virtually unlimited potential for learning and creativity. Ninety five percent of what we know about he capabilities of the human brain has been learned in the last twenty years. (Gelb, M. 1998, pg. 3).

It has been researched that "geniuses" can come from humble parents and environments that did not provide educational opportunities. Thus the theory of heredity is not applicable in all circumstances. It is this author's belief that these people are able to tap into regions of their mind, i.e. the subconscious, and do not disregard their inner thoughts as many of us do.

In the field of medicine today, we're seeing doctors embrace the power of the connection between our bodies and our minds to heal and nurture us. High-tech computer and biomedical advances are changing the face of medicine, but these breakthroughs exist hand-in-hand with a new respect for alternative medicine techniques such as biofeedback. (Robinson, L. & Finnerty, L. 1999, pg. 5).

Many disciplines are combining physical treatment with the power of the subconscious to hasten the healing process. It has been said that positive thinking is half the battle, and that means if we believe it strongly enough in our subconscious then it will become possible in our conscious lives. There are many different stigmata's attached to the methods our subconscious uses to communicate data to our conscious mind; everything from being blessed by God to having a mental illness. Perhaps this in itself is where our limitation of the knowledge awaiting us in our subconscious begins. How we perceive where the source of information comes from can decide whether or not we will explore its possibilities or block it from our conscious minds. Some people might believe that to acknowledge this inner source is to be abnormal and possibly insane. Where does this fear of being different than others come from? From past stigmas attached to concepts of normal versus abnormal. It is this author's belief that the "geniuses" of our time chose to ignore these societal labels and ventured forth by allowing their inner knowledge to surface.

Limits to the Subconscious?

The subconscious is not limited to repressed thoughts and evolutionary memories. It can do more than acquaint us with our past, it can enlighten us to many things, past, present and future. Robert Monroe, founder of the Monroe Institute of Applied Sciences, wrote in his book, *Ultimate Journey:*

> The spectrum of consciousness ranges seemingly, endlessly, beyond time-space into other energy systems. It also continues downward through animal and plant life, possibly into the subatomic level. Every human consciousness is active commonly in only a small segment of the consciousness continuum. The multimdimensionally aware can actually travel into hyperspace and have conscious visualization and perceptions of other time/space dimensions, including accessing information through their own DNA. Often they speak of formulas, mathematical equations and atomic structure in ways quite different from current scientific thought. (Bryant, A. 1998 pg. 6).

Human Limitations Placed Upon the Subconscious

There is so much power available in the universe that its potential will never be reached. This is true for knowledge as well.

I would like to call attention to an interesting remark of Immanuel Kant's. In his lectures on psychology *(Vorlesungen uber Psychologie, Leipzig, 1889)* he speaks of the "treasure lying within the field of dim representations, that deep abyss of human knowledge forever beyond our reach. (Campbell, J. 1976, footnote, pg. 119).

Due to past ideas and ways of thinking we limit our capacity for tapping into this databank of knowledge and power.

Everyone makes for himself his own segment of world and constructs his own private system, often with air-tight compartments, so that after a time it seems to him that he has grasped the meaning and structure of the whole. But the finite will never be able to grasp the infinite. (Campbell, J. 1976, pg. 23).

In the making of our private world, we put boundaries on our abilities to learn, in a book called "Quester," the author stated it in a very simple way.

"Raising our level of consciousness involves the leaving behind of our everyday senses and working outside our accepted physical laws. We need to be able to communicate with our altered state of consciousness and use its facilities for our own beliefs. (Beattie, P. 1999, pg. 1).

This writer believes that one of the first blockades to acquiring this knowledge is the denial of its existence. The second most powerful block is a belief system that we incorporate into our way of thinking that states that we are not suppose to wander into this area due to religious taboos. For some a forbidden or evil connotation has been linked with the thinking that we can communicate from within with each other and a creator.

A historical example of an extreme punishment for examining the total person is in the execution of Socrates. "Perhaps the lesson of Socrates being executed for encouraging his students to ponder "What is Self?" sufficiently scared philosophers into their ivory towers (Lesser, E. 1999, pg. 65.)."

Such punishments have led to centuries of fear of doing or participating in something that is wrong or harmful. Fear has both been responsible for forward and backward moves in our technology. Fearing to try something has halted many bright ideas from progressing and due to instinct for survival the fear of the unknown has had to be conquered and out of this has come many advancements in our universe. The fear of the unknown is one of the most powerful ingredients in failure. The excitement and quest for knowing the unknown is one of the most powerful ingredients in success.

We shall discover how great is our fear of the unconscious and how formidable are our resistances, because of these resistances we doubt the very thing that seems so obvious to the culture of the East, namely the self-liberating power of the introverted mind. (Campbell, J, 1976, pg. 490).

Carl Jung spoke of how man has rationalized himself into a state of disassociation with his inner symbols and natural universal connection.

Modern man does not understand how much his rationalism (which has destroyed his capacity to respond to numinous symbols and ideas) has put him at the mercy of the psychic *underworld*. He has freed himself from superstition or (so he believes), but in the process he has lost his spiritual values to a positively dangerous degree. His moral and spiritual tradition has disintegrated, and he is now paying the price for this break-up in world-wide disorientation and dissociation….As scientific understanding has grown, so our world has become dehumanized. Man feels himself isolated in the cosmos, because he is no longer involved in nature and has lost his emotional "unconscious identity" with natural phenomena. No voices now speak to man from stones, plants, and animals, nor does he speak to them believing they can hear. (Hergenhahn, B.R. 1990, pg. 77-78).

It is this author's firm belief that knowledge was given to us by a great creating force. Its availability has always been within our grasp, but we limit ourselves and our abilities to obtain this knowledge. A creator would not have created this ability even in a minuet sense if it were not to be available for use. We corrupt our abilities and the original purpose of existing forces in the universe by putting our own interpretation on them.

The Native Americans have always believed in a connection between the universe and man. "Naturally magnanimous and open-minded, we have always preferred to believe that the Spirit of God is not breathed into humans alone, but that the whole created universe shares in the immortal perfection of its Maker (Nerburn, K. 1999. Pg. 88)." If all share in the created universe, then we were meant to communicate with one another. If this communication were developed, think what advances in technology, society, relationships, nations, and individuals would be achieved. "Nobody, of his own free will, can strip the unconscious of its effective power. At best, one can merely deceive oneself on this point (Campbell, J. 1976, pg. 116)."

Methods of Communicating With the Subconscious

How can we tap into the vast databank of the subconscious? It has already been achieved on many levels. William Dement, Carl Jung and Sigmund Freud, among many others, agree that our dreams are a link to our subconscious mind. "Dement stated in his book "The Promise of Sleep," that anthropologists speculate that dreams first brought early humans the vision of the soul, an identity inside but separate from the body (Dement, W. 1999, pg. 28-29)." Freud believed that dreams were manifestations of suppressed thoughts and experiences. Jung was a strong believer in the theory that dreams are a connection with past events, not just the person having the dreams past, but archetypal images from generations past.

We know how important history is to our civilization. It is from history that we learn what did and did not work, and explanations for current traditions, beliefs, and practices. If dreams work to bring to the conscious past memories and events, then it is a form of enlightenment of past knowledge.

Carl Jung believed that the dream was a tool that could be used to extract the answers that humanity sought about the mysteries of life.

Jung discovered that by taking first his own and then his patients dreams and fantasies seriously, he could find the key to understanding the secret background to life; which contained hidden solutions to life's problems. It was though he had found the hidden field in which the vital missing pieces to the puzzles of people's problems lay. Jung discovered that the psyche contained its own healer which could be activated by the process of exploring dreams and fantasies. (Segaller, S. & Berger, M. 1989, pg. 40).

Freud had his theory as to the importance of the dream and its link to the subconscious.

Freud considered his book, "The Interpretation of Dreams," to be his most important contribution and it was this book that finally brought Freud the professional recognition that he had been seeking. Freud believed that it was in dreams that the contents of the unconscious were most available, still hidden, or distorted but available. Indeed, Freud thought that the Interpretation of dreams is the royal road to knowledge of the unconscious activities of the mind. (Hergenhahn, B.R. 1990, pg. 41).

Sigmund Freud theorized what he called a reflex apparatus was involved in the psychological process of memory. He believed that the apparatus is capable of memory.

Memory traces are unconscious: they can be made conscious; but there can be no doubt that they can produce all their effects while in an unconscious condition. Further additions to the model are necessary in order to account for dreams; in particular, a critical agency. This agency can exclude various ideas from consciousness, or the motor end of the apparatus; it overseas the activities of the unconscious. Dream activity is, to a certain extent, unconscious activity. (Rosenfield, I, 1970, pg. 24).

Freud incorporated the theory of F.W. Hilderbrant, who published a short book in German on dreams in 1875. Hilderbrant believed that dreams had the potential for self – disclosure. He expressed his thoughts in the following quotation:

> The dream sometimes allows us to look into the depths and folds of our very being----mainly a closed book in states of consciousness. It gives us such valuable insight into ourselves, such instructive revelations of our half-hidden emotional tendencies and powers that, were we awake, we should have good reason to stand in awe of the demon who is apparently peering at our cards with the eyes of a flacon. The dream warns from within with the voice of a watchman guarding the very center of our psychic life. It warns us against continuing on the paths which we are treading. (Castle, R.L. (1994, pg. 99).

Edgar Cayce stated in 1923, that dreams have a great influence on our conscience. One of the main themes of Cayce's theory is quoted below:

> Forget not that it has been rightly said that the Creator, the gods, and the God of the Universe speak to man through his individual self. Man approaches the more intimate condition of that field of the inner self when the conscious self is at rest in sleep. Dreams are a manifestation of the subconscious. Any (personal) condition before becoming a reality is first dreamed. (Sechrist, E. 1995, pgs. 5-7).

In our modern Western culture the significance of dreams has been merely a past time discussion for entertainment or a analytical tool used in counseling to give the Physician an idea of what troubles lie beneath the surface of the awareness of the patient. In many other cultures the dream is a relevant part of the daily lifestyle and is considered as important if not more important than awareness during the conscious state.

In many non-Western cultures, dreams are viewed as important sources of information about oneself, about the future, or about the spiritual world. Among the New Guinea Arapesh, an erotic dream about someone may be viewed as the equivalent of an adulterous act. In many cultures dreams are seen as windows into the spiritual world, permitting communication with ancestors or supernatural beings. People in some cultures believe that dreams provide information about the future. Dreaming is the focal point of traditional Aboriginal existence as it is in many other cultures. (Weiten, W. 1997, pg. 134).

Depending upon a cultures beliefs and the relevance awarded to the dream, these factors play and instrumental role in how frequently the dreamer dreams and how much they remember of their dream. "Dream recall tends to be much better in cultures that take dreams seriously (Weiten, W. 1997, pg. 134)."

The Subconscious and Conscious Together

The subconscious and conscious mind works together. The nature of the conscious is constantly active. As illustrated by figure 2. on page 20 of this paper, it shows the conscious mind's brain activity which is measured by EEG's, as having some awareness during sleep.

Your conscious mind is your awareness, your center. It thinks reasons, calculates, plans, directs all actions of your body, determines results and makes decisions. It is creative, it registers pain, fear, happiness and it sets goals (both long-term and very short-term goals). In order for the conscious mind to be able to do all of these things, it must have a place to pull information from—a storage area. The subconscious mind is our data storage bank. When our conscious mind asks our subconscious mind gives. (2000, September 9, http://www.scwleurope.com/conscious.htm).

The key to opening this vast data storage bank located in the subconscious is the awareness of its existence. We must be consciously aware in order to bring what is beneath the surface to the realm of our consciousness. This already takes place on an automated basis as stated in the above quote. What is lacking is the conscious awareness and communication between the subconscious and conscious. We are able to make this connection on an automated level, think of what could be accomplished with a conscious effort.

If we refer to the previous figure-1 on page 11 of this paper, we see that the conscious is only a small percentage of our mind, whereas the subconscious is the larger part. We are only using a small percentage of our abilities when we limit ourselves to the conscious. Effort should be made to bring more of the subconscious into communication with the conscious.

Other Methods of Communication

Other methods of communicating with our subconscious are meditation, hypnosis, biofeedback, positive thinking, and chemical induced states of conscious alteration. Meditation and hypnosis are used to quiet the conscious mind in order to allow the subconscious to be heard. "Meditation refers to a family of mental exercises in which a conscious attempt is made to focus attention in a non-analytical way. Of interest to psychology is the fact that meditation involves a deliberate effort to alter consciousness (Weiten, W. 1997, pg. 138)." Meditation became somewhat of a "fad" in the 1960's. Zen Buddhism and Yoga were popular practices being introduced in the United States. Seminars and training programs in these Eastern beliefs were very popular.

Hypnosis is another method used to allow the subconscious to be contacted on a more direct basis. In the hypnotic state, the person is focused on a narrowed area of thought, thereby limiting conscious mental activity. Hypnotism and its benefits have been woven into history and folklore for many years. Many theories state that hypnosis is an altered state of consciousness.

Ernest Hilgard theorized that divided consciousness is a common, normal experience. For example, people will often drive a car a great distance, responding to traffic signals and other cars, with no recollection of having consciously done so. Interestingly, this common experience has long been known as highway hypnosis. (Weiten, W. 1997, pg. 138).

Another popular method of mind communication is biofeedback. This involves a form of consciously programming your mind to affect your body.

Biofeedback techniques were developed to bring body systems involving factors such as blood pressure or temperature under voluntary control by providing feedback from the body, so that subjects could learn to control their responses. For example, researchers found that persons could control their brain-wave patterns to some extent, particularly the so-called alpha rhythms generally associated with a relaxed, meditative state. This was especially relevant to those interested in consciousness and meditation, and a number of alpha training programs emerged. (Microsoft Encarta 2000, *Interest in Altered States IV.* Pg. 2).

Positive thinking is used to tell your subconscious what you want it to do. Prayer and faith are an example of positive thought. If one believes in something strongly on a conscious level, repeated practice and belief will be instilled into the subconscious. These beliefs would be transmitted through the subconscious from one generation to the next according to the theory of archetypes by Carl Jung.

Positive thinking has become a part of the business world in more ways than one. Many companies use training seminars to teach their employees the importance of a positive attitude. Executives take courses on the benefits of having a positive attitude and transmitting that to their employees. On the other end of business, it has become a profitable venture for many. There are self-help books, tapes, videos, seminars, and television shows as well as info commercials selling products about positive thinking.

Chemical alteration can be used to quiet or alter a person's conscious thoughts, thus allowing a more active subconscious to express itself. Alcohol, marijuana, and other "recreational drugs" are some common means of inducing this altered state. This can have a negative effect by interrupting the pure form of subconscious communication. The knowledge being transferred from the subconscious to the conscious is corrupted. This chemical alteration can cause permanent damage to a person's physical body as well as his mental thought processes. Perhaps this could account for heredity psychosis. If everything is in the mind, including the past, then the minds that have been corrupted pass that misinformation on to the next generation.

Divisions of the Mind

The Hawaiian Islands Huna teachings state that the human being is made up of three selves, or minds. They can most easily be called the subconscious mind, the conscious mind, and the super conscious mind. The third part is the high self, called the "aumakua" and is the older utterly trustworthy parental self of spirit. It will not interfere in the affaires of life unless asked to do so. (2000, August 25, http://www.crystalinks.com/huna.html).

According to the Huna belief system, the Aumakua is able to see into the future as far as your thoughts have been crystallized.

An American psychologist, Edward Bradford Titchener from Cornell University developed an introspective approach on describing the structure of the mind. "Titchener attempted to detail, from introspective self-reports, the dimensions of the elements of consciousness. For example, taste was "dimensionalized" into four basic categories: sweet, sour, salt, and bitter. This approach was known as structuralism (Microsoft Encarta, 2000, *Foundations of Modern Research*, pg. 1)."

Carl Jung developed a chart that described his belief upon the divisions of the mind, and the universal connection. He stated that many cultures had symbols to represent this subconscious connection. These were evidence of a collective unconscious. According to his chart the mind also had three divisions: The conscious, personal conscious, and the collective unconscious.

Figure 4. (Weiten, W. 1997, pg. 337)

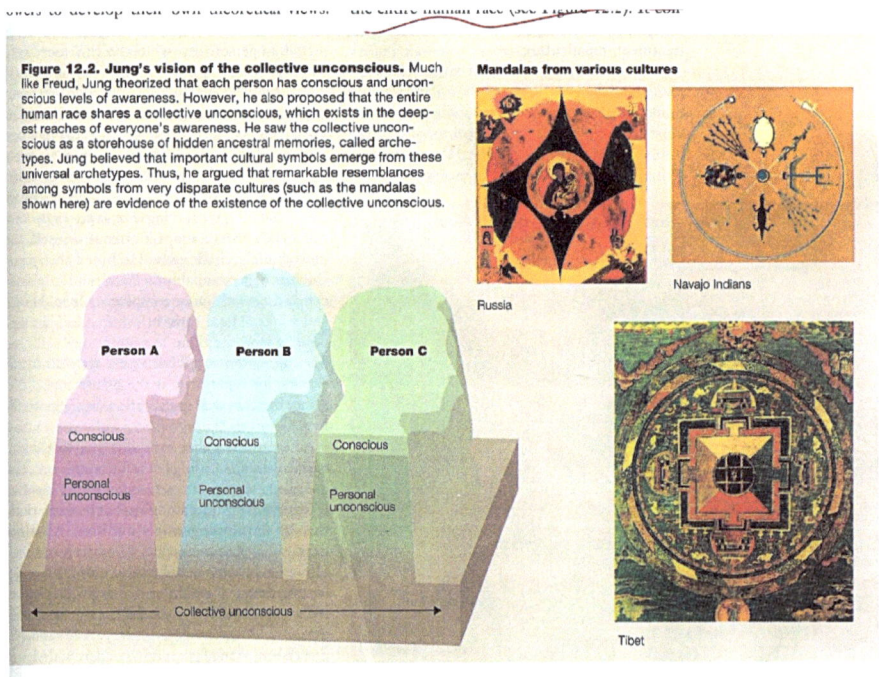

Weiten, W. (1997). Psychology Themes and Variations 3rd Ed. New York: Brooks/Cole Publishing. Pg. 337. Chart 12.2.

There is no dispute among scholars and theorists about the mind having more than one aspect; the dispute comes regarding what those divisions are and how they work together.

Conclusion

History tells us that man has had a belief of communication with a deity and with fellow man since the most ancient of times. The Indians believed in spirits in the sky earth, animals and man. They believed these spirits communicated with them through vision quests or other rituals. The Egyptians believed in an afterlife where the soul continues to live its life, and they believed in the foretelling of future events. Christians believe in prophets, and divine messages. Metaphysics or the 0ccult believe in a divine power working through gifted persons. These different belief systems have a common thread running through their makeup.

Most surveys suggest that about a third of the general population have had a "weak" mystical experience at some time in their lives. This survey also found that mystical experiences were more common in people whose lives already had some spiritual dimension, for example, people who regularly prayed or meditated. What is surprising is that people who are active members of a church or synagogue were less likely to report such experiences. (Fenwick, P. & Fenwick, E. 1998, pgs. 268-269).

The quest for knowledge and new experiences has led many to search for alternative answers. The answers along with an outstanding life changing experience are within the person if they know how to communicate with their inner being.

The subconscious mind takes in everything we learn and experience in our lifetime. It begins at birth (some say before birth), soaking up information like a sponge, accumulating data as we grow and experience life. It also begins forming beliefs based on what we learn and what we experience, which determines how we react to everything in our life. These beliefs gain both strength and momentum the older we become. (2000, September 9, http://www.scwleurope.com/conscious.htm).

This same article quotes Mildred Man in saying "nothing will happen to change your life until you consciously step in and start to work with the subconscious mind, otherwise, you will continue in the same pattern you have built up (2000, September 9, http://www.scwleurope.com/conscious.htm)."

The subconscious is many things, who is to say where our inspirations, messages, and insight comes from. They have always been with us and will always be available to us; we are the only thing standing between the known and the unknown.

Infinite riches are all around you if you will open your mental eyes and behold the treasure house of infinity within you. There is a gold mine within you from which you can extract everything you need to live life gloriously, joyously, and abundantly. (Murphy, J. 1963, p. 19).

References

Armstrong, K. (2000). The Battle for God. New York: Alfred A. Knopf.

Beattie, P. (1999). Quester: The Journey of the Brave. MA: Shaftesbury.

Blackburn, S. (1999). Think. Oxford: Oxford University Press.

Brady, L. St. Lifer, Evan. (1998). Discovering Your Soul Mission. New York: Three Rivers Press.

Breathnach, S. (1998). Something More: Excavating Your Authentic Self. New York: Warner Books.

Bryant, A. , & Seebach, L. (1998). Human Multidimensional Potential. New York: Wildflower Press.

Bucke, R. (1961). Cosmic Consciousness: A Study in the Evolution of the Human Mind. Concord, Mass: Ye old Department Press.

Castle, R.L. (1994). Our Dreaming Mind. New York: Ballantine Books.

Campbell, J. (Ed.) (1976). The Portable JUNG. New York: Penguin Books.

Chaffee, J. (1998). The Thinkers Way. New York: Little, Brown, & Company.

Cheetham, E. (1989). The Final Prophecies of Nostradamus. New York: Pedigree Books.

"Consciousness, States of," Microsoft Encarta Online Encyclopedia 2000. http://encarta.msn.com 1997-2000 Microsoft Corporation.

Coopersmith, S. (1966). Frontiers of Psychological Research. San Francisco: W.H. Freeman and CO.

Cox, David. (1968). <u>Modern Psychology: The Teachings of Carl Gustav Jung.</u> New York: Barnes & Noble.

Davies, P. (1999). <u>The Fifth Miracle: The Search for the Origin and Meaning of Life.</u> New York: Simon & Shuster.

DE Laszlo, V.S. (Ed.). (1991). <u>Psyche and Symbol.</u> N.J: Princeton University Press.

Dement, W., & Vaughn, C. (1999). <u>The Promise of Sleep.</u> New York: Delacorte Press.

Denning & Phillips. (1997). <u>The Development of Psychic Powers.</u> MN: Llewellyn Publications.

Ehrman, B. (2000). <u>The New Testament: A Historical Introduction to the Early Christian Writings.</u> (2nd Ed). New York: Oxford Press.

Erdoes, R., & Ortiz, A. (Eds.). (1984). <u>American Indian Myths & Legends.</u> New York: Pantheon Books.

Fenwick, P. & Fenwick, E. (1999) <u>The Hidden Door: Understanding and Controlling Dreams.</u> New York: Berkley Books.

Ferguson, R. (1979). <u>Universal Mind.</u> New Jersey: Prentice Hall.

Flowers, B.S. (Ed.). (1988). <u>Joseph Campbell: The Power of Myth, with Bill Moyers.</u> New York: Doubleday.

Fordham, F. (1988). <u>An Introduction to Jung's Psychology.</u> LA: Pelican.

Freud, S. (1958). <u>On Creativity and the Unconscious.</u> New York: Harper and Row.

Gelb, M. (1998). How to think Like Leonardo Da Vinci: Seven Steps to Genius Everyday. New York: Delacorte Press.

Godwin, M. (2000). Who Are You? New York: Penguin.

Goleman, D. (1994). Emotional Intelligence. New York: Bantam Books.

Goleman, D. (1998). Working With Emotional Intelligence. New York: Bantam Books.

Grackenbach, J. , & Laberge, S., (Eds.). (1988). Conscious Mind, Sleeping Brain: Perspectives on Lucid Dreaming. New York: Plenium.

Gyatso, G.K. (1999). Introduction to Buddhism. London: Tharpa Publications.

Hale, D. & Hale, R.E., (1995). Caring For The Mind: The Comprehensive guide to Mental Health. New York: Bantam Books.

Hamilton, E. (1942). Mythology. Mass: Little Brown & Co.

Hearne, K. (1984, February). A Survey of Reported Premonitions and of Those Who Have Them. Journal of the Society for Psychology Research. (52. No. 796).

Hergenhahn, B.R. (1990). An Introduction to Theories of Personality. New Jersey: Prentice Hall.

Higher Awareness: Intuition Awareness and Psychic Development. (2000). Awareness and Intuition. http://www.higherawareness.com/awarenessand intuition.shtml. (2000, August 25).

Hirschfelder, A. (2000). Native Americans: A History in Pictures. New York: Dorling Kindersley Publishing, Inc.

Holmes, E. (1998). The Science of the Mind. New York: Penguin Putnam Inc.

Holmes, E. (2000). <u>What Is the Science of Mind.</u>

http://www.religiousscience.org/whatissom1.htm   (2000, September 9).

James, P., & Thorpe, N. (1999). <u>Ancient Mysteries.</u> New York: Ballantine Books.

Jung, C.G. (1965). <u>Memories, Dreams, Reflections.</u> New York: Random House.

Kingsolver, B. (1990). <u>Animal Dreams.</u> New York: Harper Perennial.

Kornfield, J. (2000). <u>After The Ecstasy The Laundry.</u> New York: Bantam.

Kowalski, G. (1991). <u>The Souls of Animals.</u> NH: Stillpoint Publishing.

Lesser, E. (1999). <u>The New American Spirituality.</u> New York: Random House.

Margolis, C. (1999). <u>Questions From Earth Answers From Heaven.</u> New York: St. Martin Press.

Martin, T. (1997). <u>Psychic and Paranormal Phenomena in The Bible.</u> TN: Psychicpace.

Miller, K. (1999). <u>Finding Darwin's God.</u> New York: Cliff Street Books.

Murphy, J. (1968). <u>The Cosmic Power Within You.</u> New Jersey: Prentice Hall.

Murphy, J. (1963). <u>The Power of Your Subconscious Mind.</u> New Jersey: Prentice Hall.

Myss, C. (1996). <u>Anatomy of the Spirit.</u> New York: Three Rivers Press.

Naparster, B. (1997). <u>Your Sixth Sense: Activating Your Psychic Potential.</u> CA. Harper Collins.

Nerburn, K. (Ed.). (1999). <u>The Wisdom of the Native Americans.</u> CA: New World Library.

Newton, M. (1999). <u>Journey of Souls.</u> MN: Llewellyn Publications.

Nichols, S. (1980). Jung and Tarot: An Archetypal Journey. MA: Samuel Weiser.

Ornish, D. (1998). Love & Survival: The Scientific Basis for the Healing Power of Intimacy. New York: Harper Collins Pub.

Ornstein, R., & Thompson, R.F. (1984). The Amazing Brain. MASS: Houghton Miffin.

Parrinder, G. (Ed.). (1971). World Religions: From Ancient History to Present. New York: Facts on File Publications.

Peirce, P. (1997). The Intuitive Way. Oregon: Beyond Worlds Publishing.

Pelikan, J. (Ed.). (1992). Sacred Writings The Qur'an. New York: Book of the Month Club.

Penrose, R. (1994). Shadows of the Mind: A Search for the Missing Science of Consciousness. New York: Oxford University Press.

Pettijohn, T.F. (1992). Psychology. Connecticut: The Dalkin Publishing Group.

Ramachandran, V.S., & Blakeslee, S. (1998). Phantoms In The Brain: Probing the Mysteries Of The Human Mind. New York: William Morrow.

Redfield, J. (1993). The Celestine Prophecy. New York: Warner Books.

Reid, J. (2000) Ernest Holmes: The First Religious Scientist. http://www.religiousscience.org/firstrs1.htm. (2000, September 9).

Richards, L. (1993). Baffling Bible Questions Answered. New York: Testament Books.

Richards, L. (1991). The Bible Readers Companion: Your Guide to Every Chapter of The Bible. MD: Ottenheimer Publishers.

Ritberger, C. (1998). Your Personality Your Health. CA: Hay House.

Robinson, L.A., & Finnerty, L.C. (1999). The Complete Idiot's Guide to Being

Psychic. New York: Alpha Books.

Rosen, S., (Ed.). (2000). The Examined Life. New York: Random House.

Rosenfield, I. (1970). Freud: Character and Consciousness. New York:

University Books.

Rush, J.H. (1962). The Dawn Of Life. New York: New American Library.

Sagan, C. (1980). Cosmos. New York: Random House.

Sagan, C. (1977). The Dragons of Eden/Speculations on the Evolution of Human

Intelligence. New York: Ballantine Books.

Schulz, M.L. (1998). Awakening Intuition. New York: Harmony Books.

Sechrist, E. (1995). Dreams Your Magic Mirror. New York: Gramercy Books.

Segaller, S. & Berger, M. (1989). The Wisdom of the Dream. Boston:

Shambhala Publications.

Shermer, M. (2000). How We Believe: The Search for God in an Age of Science.

New York: WittFreeman.

Smoley, R., & Kinnery, J. (1999). Hidden Wisdom. New York: Penguin Group.

Snith, J. (Ed.). (1998). Breath Sweeps Mind. New York: Riverhead Books.

Snuit, M. (1999). The Soul Bird. New York: Hyperion.

Stone, J.D. (2000). Huna Teachings:Hidden Mysteries.

http://www.crystalinks.com/huna.html. (2000, August 25).

Stumpf, S. (1994). Philosophy: History and Problems. New York: McGraw Hill.

The Conscious and Subconscious Mind. (2000). The Subconscious Mind.

http://www.scwleurope.com/conscious.htm (2000, August 26).

The Power of the Subconscious Mind. (2000) The Subconscious Mind?

http://www.ascc.org/library/art11.html (2000, August 25).

The Super-Subconscious Mind. (1996).

http://www.lightparty.com/Health/SuperSub.html (2000, August 25).

Til, C.V. (1966). An Introduction To Systematic Theology. Philadelphia:

Westminster Theological Seminary.

Titmuss, C. (1999). The Power of Meditation. New York: Sterling Publishing Co.

Weiten, W. (1997). Psychology Themes and Variations 3rd Ed. New York:

Brooks/Cole Publishing.

White, E.G. (1971). The Great Controversy. Boise: Pacific Press.

Wilson, J.R. (1969). The Mind New York: Time-Life Books

Wilkinson, P. (1999). Illustrated Dictionary Religions. New York: DK Publishing

Books.

Wise, E. (2000). Letter to Earth: Who We Are Becoming And What We Need to

Know. New York: Harmony Books.

Zukav, G. (1990). The Seat of the Soul. New York: Simon & Shuster.

Figures Obtained From:

Figure 1

Thom, Loretta (2000). <u>Designed by Clipart from Word and Coloring and Assembly by Loretta Thom.</u>

Figure 2

Weiten, W. (1997). <u>Psychology Themes and Variations 3rd Ed.</u> New York: Brooks/Cole Publishing. Pg. 126, Chart 5.5 EEG.

Figure 3

<u>The New Book of Knowledge: The Children's Encyclopedia.</u> (1967) New York: Groiler. Vol. 16, pg. 71.

Figure 4

Weiten, W. (1997). <u>Psychology Themes and Variations 3rd Ed.</u> New York: Brooks/Cole Publishing. Pg. 337. Chart 12.2.